A Practical Guide to Insurance & Employee Benefits

A Start in Understanding Your Core and Supplemental Benefit Offerings

By Donna V. Werner

Insurance Consultant, Benefit Counselor, Licensed Insurance Agent, & Trusted Business Advisor

Contents

Why this guide?

In my work as a benefit counselor, I have had the opportunity to meet with thousands of employees in every industry, with employers large and small to meet across the table and sometimes with a laptop on my chair to discuss employee benefits on behalf of a company.

Some of the same questions arise again and again, even aside from the fact that the average person has no clue what is part of their worksite employee benefit portfolio.

As an educator at heart, and someone who worked 15 years in higher education, I understand the importance of education in every area, especially when you think about the importance of benefits, insurance, and the ways that those products are intended to protect families, homes, and futures.

This book is intended to be a practical guide you can use, even if you never get the chance to sit down with someone like me who can help you personalize the information to your families' situation. You will find worksheets, definitions, questions for you to answer honestly and sincerely. Since the guide is for your personal use and you don't have to share the answers with anyone, <u>PLEASE be as honest with yourself as you can</u>.

If you have additional questions you can connect with me directly on Facebook, LinkedIn, or Twitter. If you are interested, we can even meet via Skype or FaceTime for a consultation. Visit my website or reach out with your questions and comments -- www.WernerBusinessGroup.com; (708) 330-5383; Donna@WernerBusinessGroup.com; @WernerBizGroup. I am also interested in your feedback on the book AND to know if there is something you wish I would have covered that is not in the book.

Either way, I hope you will find this book interesting, educational, informative, and helpful to you and your family, regardless of what stage of life or career you are in.

Here we go!

Disclaimer: This glossary of terms is intended to offer a simple way to provide a general understanding of the concepts, though NOT intended to serve as formal definitions. Remember...the purpose of this book is for you to understand how these benefits/products might work for you, your family, your household, your budget, and your situation.

Glossary:

PLEASE NOTE: The terms are not listed in order of importance or in any particular priority order.

Employer-sponsored/paid life insurance – **Some employers pay for life insurance that is for an employee only during the time of their employment. This means that if an employee dies while they are actively on payroll, their family will receive proceeds from that employer-sponsored/paid life insurance policy. The amount the family will receive is decided by the employer and can be whatever amount they decide or a multiple of the employee's salary. This is the type of insurance that does NOT go with the employee if they leave the company/employer. The employer owns and controls the policy. Individual employees can be issued a certificate showing what the agreement is.**

Employee Benefits – **According to the internet, a benefit is an advantage or profit you gain from something. In the of employee benefits, you gain certain things from your employer because you work there. Those benefits may be everything from sick leave and vacation pay to insurance products like medical, dental, and life insurance. Different employers offer different "benefits" to their employees.**

Life insurance – **In some cases life insurance can more realistically be considered "death insurance" because someone might have to die for the proceeds to be available for use. I say "might" have to die because there are types of life insurance that do not require for you to die for you to have funds available to you. Those benefits are called "living benefits."**

Term Insurance – The simplest way to describe term insurance is to say that it is temporary. It will go away at some point in time. It is generally not the type of insurance you keep into old age. It is like renting insurance since you do not permanently own it. Some people purchase term insurance intending to keep it into old age but get surprised when they see how much the cost goes up over time.

Universal Insurance – Universal is a type of permanent insurance that can allow you to pay flexible premiums, rather than a constant, fixed monthly amount. Be careful, though, because if you only pay the minimum premium, it can expire just like term insurance.

Indexed Universal Life – Indexed life insurance products capture the gains of the stock market without subjecting you to the potential losses of the stock market. Many indexed universal life products have very high cash value inside the policy that can be used as a living benefit for savings, retirement, etc., and since it is life insurance, it also has a death benefit to be passed on to your beneficiaries.

Fixed vs Variable – Fixed products have a set interest rate compared to variable products which can go up and down, based on stock market conditions.

Disability Insurance – True "paycheck protection." Disability insurance is a percentage of your gross income that you can receive if you have a medical disability that is confirmed by a doctor/medical professional. Disability insurance is something that can either be employer-paid or purchased/owned by the employee.

Short-term Disability – Short-term disability insurance is the initial period of a disability. It can be as soon as the 1st day of an accident and the 7th day of a sickness/surgery or as long as weeks or months after the disability begins.

Short-term disability, like term life insurance, ends at a certain point in time, e.g., 3-6 months up to 2 years.

Long-term Disability – Depending on multiple factors, long-term disability can start as soon as 3 months after the beginning of the health incident, BUT long-term disability can potentially take you up to retirement age or the end of the disability...whichever comes first. The key is to make it through the first, initial period of the disability. Many people forego short-term disability because they do not realize that they have to get through the first part of their medical crisis.

Employer-paid – Employer-paid is just like it sounds; the employer pays for the benefit. Therefore, since the employer is paying for it, they make the decisions about what it is. It most cases, if the employer pays for "it," the employer also owns "it."

Voluntary/Supplemental Benefits – These benefits are generally insurance products that the employee himself/herself owns and controls. Supplemental benefits are payroll-deducted, i.e., come right out of your paycheck. The employer will allow a certain vendor/provider/carrier to offer these benefits to each individual employee so they can customize a benefit that will fit their budget, family structure, and priorities. Supplemental benefits pay directly to the employee apart from any other insurance or benefits they have. Whereas medical, dental, vision insurance pays providers of care, supplemental benefits pay the employee/patient.

Portability/Portable – Portable products are voluntary/supplemental benefits that go with the employee when they leave the employer due to termination, separation, resignation, retirement. Everything remains the same, with no change in cost or design. The only thing that changes is how the benefit is paid for, i.e., going from payroll deduction to direct bill or EFT.

Convertibility/Convertible – A convertible product is usually a life insurance product that can be modified from one type to another. It can also be a product that is a group product that can be modified to an individual one. In many cases, the price goes up because the benefit design goes up. An example would be a term life insurance plan you get through your employer being converted to a whole life insurance product when you retire. You will pay the price according to your current age, not the age when you first purchased it.

Accident Insurance – A supplemental benefit payable directly to you based on an injury caused by an accident. The internet defines an accident as an unfortunate incident that happens unexpectedly and unintentionally, typically resulting in damage or injury. Accident insurance has a pre-determined benefit schedule based on the injury itself and how it is treated. Usually you are paid for things like ambulance, hospitalization, x-rays, burns, cuts, surgery, and more.

Accidental Death & Dismemberment (AD&D) – Sometimes referred to as double indemnity. AD&D can be a standalone benefit or it can be added to another plan as a rider. It pays for death-by-injury or loss of limb. AD&D typically doubles the death benefit. If you only have AD&D insurance, it will not pay for death by natural causes.

Critical Illness Insurance – This supplemental benefit pays usually a lump sum benefit upon diagnosis of illnesses like heart attack, stroke, kidney failure, organ transplant that are explicitly detailed in the benefit brochure or outline of coverage. Different carriers have different plan designs that offer different lump sum payment amounts and may also pay by illness categories. Critical illness plans generally pay a wellness or health screening benefit after you have had your annual check-up.

Cancer Insurance – Depending on the company/carrier, this supplemental benefit either pays for various treatments or a lump sum benefit upon diagnosis of cancer. The money pays directly to the patient/person diagnosed with cancer. It also generally pays a wellness or health screening benefit every year after you get a check-up or have certain medical testing done. You will use your medical insurance to pay for the testing and inform the cancer insurance carrier after-the-fact.

Deductible – One of the out-of-pocket expenses you will incur with medical insurance plans. Your deductible must be met annually/during every 12-month period before your co-insurance cost-sharing begins with the insurance company. Contrary to popular opinion, you do NOT have to pay the deductible in one payment. It will accumulate as you are utilizing your medical insurance and paying smaller bills during the course of your plan year.

Co-pay/co-payment – You will have co-pays when you have medical insurance. The co-payment is a payment to doctor or other medical provider, pharmacy, etc. to utilize their service on your behalf. The co-payment is your share of the cost, according to the plan benefit design contract. The insurance company pays the other part of the bill on your behalf.

Premium – The premium is the ongoing payment you will make for your insurance benefit. Depending on the type of insurance/benefit, the premium will remain the same indefinitely, change at some point in time, or stop at some point in time.

Final expense/funeral/burial insurance – These terms are sometimes used interchangeably when looking at a smaller life insurance plan. These types of plans can pay as little as $1,000 up to about $20,000 or $25,000 when the insured dies. In most cases, the death benefit proceeds can be designated to go to a person, a funeral home, an estate, or other entity.

Mortgage protection insurance – **Mortgage protection is usually a self-owned life insurance policy so that the family of the insured or mortgage-holder will have money to use to pay off the house/property/dwelling upon the death of the insured. In most cases a term life insurance product is used because the mortgage is for a pre-defined length of time. IMPORTANT NOTE: It is up to the insured/mortgage-holder to be clear about the purpose of this life insurance since the beneficiary will be the one to receive the proceeds after the insured dies. The money will NOT go directly to the mortgage company until there is a legal document in place to make this directive.**

PMI (Private Mortgage Insurance) – **PMI is not the same as mortgage protection insurance. PMI protects the bank if you default on your loan. To my knowledge, it is not something you can purchase on your own.**

Group vs individual insurance – **You can sometimes get a lower rate by getting insurance through your employer instead of on your own, because insurance companies look at the employees as a group, rather than at you as a single person. Sometimes the rates are better, sometime they won't ask you medical questions. You can always try to get the same type of coverage directly with an insurance company, but they will likely ask more questions and be more invasive. You will also NOT get the benefit of having your premiums payroll-deducted. Many people like that as an option because you do not have to worry about forgetting to send in payments, bank account being overdrawn and similar reasons why coverages lapse.**

Hospital indemnity – **Hospitalization indemnity plans pay you directly for being admitted to the hospital for treatment or observation. This is NOT the same as going to the emergency room and waiting a long time. You must have a bed assigned to you, with at least an overnight stay. Different plans also might pay for doctor visits, outpatient/day surgery and other benefits. Look at your plan summary/detail to find out whether you will receive a flat payment regardless of the number of days you stay or get paid based on the number of days you stay in.**

Wellness benefit – **A wellness benefit is what I consider something like a "rebate." Your supplemental benefits might include a wellness benefit that will pay you anywhere from $25 and up for having a certain type of test. The benefit pays you directly AFTER you had whatever testing qualifies for the benefit. Remember that since supplemental benefits are separate from your medical insurance, you will need to file a claim via phone, internet, paper...to request the benefit.**

Individual vs. dependent/family coverage – **Employers will often pay for employees' benefits and allow the employee to pay for his/her own dependent plans. The employer will decide how much and whether they will pay for any of the employee's family and to what extent. If you have family, you will have to decide whether you will pay for their insurance through the worksite or on your own. Your employer might have different "tiers," whether employee, employee plus one (The "one" can be spouse or a child.), family (Any 2 or more dependents). Supplemental benefits will have similar designations, allowing you to determine who to cover on which plans.**

Rider – **An add-on to an insurance product where you can cover dependents, usually spouse, children, grandchildren for a very low cost. When your dependents are covered with a rider, if you stop/cancel/terminate your own plan, they will lose coverage since you are covered as a "package."**

Out-of-pocket expenses – These are costs you will directly pay from either your paycheck or your own funds for the benefit of having medical insurance. Traditional/usual out-of-pocket expenses include your medical insurance premium, co-pays, deductibles, etc. Other costs you might not have thought about include loss of salary (for yourself or spouse/significant other/family) from time off work to care for yourself or family, travel/transportation costs, wheelchairs, crutches, bandages, over-the-counter medicine that medical insurance won't pay for, etc. Many of these costs are not covered by insurance and must be covered somehow.

Out-of-pocket maximum – The most you will pay in a 12-month period during your plan year to pay for utilization of your medical insurance plan. The out-of-pocket maximum can be the same as your deductible or can be much higher. Look at your medical insurance plan design for details.

Why do I need supplemental insurance? Doesn't my health insurance pay for "that?"

One confusing thing for people is the understanding of why they might need supplemental (also known as "voluntary" benefits). There are several reasons for you to consider.

The first is that, supplemental insurance provides a way for you to pay for the costs that your health insurance does not.

Even if you have medical insurance, there are a number of costs that you pay for, including: the premium, copays, deductibles, out of pocket maximums, PLUS any time off of work to care for yourself, your children, your spouse, and transportation costs to doctor visits. You can pay for these costs several ways, also...using money set aside for other bills, savings, retirement fund proceeds, borrowing money from friends or family or a neighborhood provider of loans e.g., title loans stores, pawn shops, etc.

Having a supplemental benefit product or two will allow you to have money to pay those unexpected, unplanned-for costs AND/OR to replace any monies you did have to borrow. Because supplemental benefits are insurance, like your medical insurance is, you will pay regular, small payments to keep your plan in place. Supplemental insurance provides you with a financial safety net so you do not have a financial emergency when you have a medical emergency.

Possible typical supplemental benefits

- Critical illness
- Cancer
- Accident
- Short/long-term disability
- Hospital indemnity
- Dental
- Vision
- Life insurance (term, whole, universal)
- ....and more...

We consider these benefits supplemental because due to the U.S. laws around the Affordable Care Act, medical insurance is the only one that is mandated by the government. However, you still have the option to pay the penalty if you choose not to have medical insurance. Should you choose that route, you will not only have to pay the penalty, but you will also be faced with any medical bills you incur. For up-to-date information on the laws and restrictions related to the Affordable Care Act visit the US Internal Revenue Service website at irs.gov.

What should I consider when thinking about which benefits I should obtain?

The following questions are not in order of importance, they are simply intended to give you real questions that are important in your decision-making process.

When was the last time OR have you ever sat down with someone to review your individual benefit plan and insurance coverages?

Do you REALLY know what's coming out of your paycheck?

Do you REALLY know how to use the benefits you are paying for?

What is your medical insurance deductible and how much of that money do you have readily available in your bank account?

If you had to come up with a lump sum of cash quickly, where would it come from?

How much sick leave/paid time off/employer salary continuation benefits do you have? Do you tend to use your sick leave a lot or only when absolutely necessary?

How much do you have in savings, in case of an emergency?

How much do you have available on your credit card?

How much can you borrow from friends/coworkers/relatives in case you need a loan?

How long could you live comfortably without a paycheck?

How much are your ongoing monthly bills? What is the total of your fixed and variable monthly expenses?

Do you have children who often need your care because of sicknesses/accidents?

Are you part of a one-income or two-income household? What would happen if one of those incomes were gone?

Do you have a health condition (e.g., high blood pressure, high cholesterol, diabetes) or lifestyle (e.g., smoking, excessive drinking, high risk hobbies) that could result in a sudden illness or accident?

Do you have a spouse who might need you to care for them if they were to have a major illness or accident?

What would happen if you had a prescription that would cost you $150 or more per month?

How would you and your family's lifestyle change if there was a sudden medical crisis?

Do you have life insurance outside of your job? If so, what kind is it? Is it subject to change/end? If it is term, will you get your money back at the end of the term?

When was the last time you reviewed your life insurance plan?

When was the last time you updated your beneficiaries?

How much do you have in your retirement savings portfolio?

What types of retirement savings plans do you currently have? Are they all in the stock market (i.e., 401k, 403b, mutual funds)?

How much of your retirement savings is available to you prior to retirement age?

How much money has your retirement savings plan lost in the past 1-10 years?

The following are a sample of worksheets I use when working with clients... If you want actual quotes, contact me to answer the questions OR just complete the worksheets and send them to me.

Life Insurance Data Sheet –

If you like a quote, complete and submit to Donna@WernerBusinessGroup.com

Gender   male female   Smoker   yes no

Birthday_____   Height_____

    Weight_____

Medications_____

Health conditions being treated for_____

Email address you want your quote sent to_____

Phone _____

Type of life insurance to quote *(circle all that apply)*

     5 year term 10 year term   20 year term   30 year term

     Return of Premium term Whole life   Indexed   Universal

Face amount/death benefit: $_____

Will this insurance be used to replace existing insurance?   Yes   No

Have you been denied insurance in the past?   Yes   No

Which riders do you want added: *(circle all that apply)*

    Critical Illness   Waiver of Premium   Accelerated Death Benefit

    Disability

Comments or questions: _____

CONFIDENTIAL WEALTH ACCUMULATION SURVEY

1. Have you lost any money in the Stock Market (via stocks, mutual funds, etc.) in the past five years?

    Yes   No   Don't know

2. How comfortable are you with your emergency savings plan?

    Extremely comfortable   Somewhat Comfortable   What emergency savings plan??

3. Which type of retirement savings do you own? *(circle all that apply)*

Mutual Funds	IRA/SEP	401k/403b
Stocks/Bonds	Deferred Comp	TSP
CD's	Pension	Annuities
Other	None	

4. Do you currently have a savings plan with a GUARANTEED rate of return?

    Yes   No   Don't know

5. Date of Birth_____ Age_____

6. At what age are you planning to retire? _____

7. Are you contributing to any savings/retirement plans? Yes   No

8. Do you know where your retirement income will come from? Yes   No

9. How much would you like to have accumulated by retirement?

    $_____

10.   How much of this do you have so far? $_____

11.   Subtract 65 (or proposed retirement age) from your current age to calculate the amount of years left to retire. _____

12.   Divide the years left to retire by the amount shown for question 10. This will show you how much you need to save to have the amount shown on line 9. $_____

13.   Email address and phone number you want to use to communicate:

_____

Your Financial Worksheet

Think about and write down any savings goals you have and the amount you need to save.

My savings goals: What do I want to save money for?? Examples might be for emergencies, education for children, retirement, etc.

$_____

_____

$_____

_____

$_____

_____

$_____

_____

Write down some ways to save money for the goals you identify.

Strategies to save for my goals: Examples might be to stop smoking, take lunch at least 1 day per week, get a part-time job, have a garage/yard sale, etc.

_____

_____

_____

_____

_____

_____

_____

_____

Write down WHY it is important to develop/create savings and financial goals for yourself and your family. Examples might be: to develop discipline and self-control, to provide a legacy of saving for your children, etc.

_____

_____

_____

_____

_____

_____

Donna V. Werner

Werner Business Group

Donna@WernerBusinessGroup.com

www.WernerBusinessGroup.com

Copyright © 2015